THE NEW LIFE LIBRARY

LOVE CHARMS

THE NEW LIFE LIBRARY

LOVE CHARMS

SPELLS OF ENCHANTMENT TO ENTICE AND KEEP A LOVER

LAURA J. WATTS

This edition first published by Hermes House,
an imprint of Anness Publishing Limited
Hermes House, 88–89 Blackfriars Road,
London SE1 8HA

Published in the USA by Hermes House,
Anness Publishing Inc.
27 West 20th Street,
New York, NY 10011

A CIP catalogue record for this book is
available from the British Library.

Publisher: Joanna Lorenz
Senior editor: Doreen Palamartschuk
Designers: Tania Monckton and Ian Sandom
Photographer: Don Last
Illustrator: Lucinda Ganderton
Indexer: Janet Smy
Editorial reader: Jan Cutler

Previously published as *Love Charms*

10 9 8 7 6 5 4 3 2 1

CONTENTS

INTRODUCTION 6

The Art of Giving 8

The Art of Receiving 9

Legendary Love Charms 10

Fairytale Love Charms 12

Courting Charms 14

Marriage Charms 16

Tokens for Love Charms 18

THE CYCLE OF LOVE 26

Season of Dreams 28

Dream Catcher Love Charm 32

Dream Space Love Charm 34

Season of Hope 36

Maypole Love Charm 40

Wishing Stone Love Charm 42

Season of Passion 44

Garland Love Charm 48

Eternity Band Love Charm 50

Season of Fulfilment 52

Protective Love Charm 56

Talking Stick Love Charm 58

Final Word 60

Table of Symbols 62

Index 64

INTRODUCTION

To love someone is to give wholeheartedly, without expectation, and to receive openly, without judgement or reservation. Only your true self can love in this way. When ego or cynicism does not weigh you down, when you are not living in the past or in an imagined future, then you are at peace with yourself and can love.

Love represents the heart, not the mind, and it can often defy the boundaries of reason. Love can express raw emotions, uncut and untempered by logic or analysis. It does not exist just to please another or yourself, it simply is.

Love is universal and connects all things. You need only to open your heart to feel the wellspring of love around you. Love charms are gifts that honour both your and your connection with the universe. That connection may be romantic love, sisterly love or the love for an animal or flower. Making a love charm, filling its creation with your hopes, not your fantasies, with your unconditional love, not your desires, reminds you of who you are and where you are going.

A love charm is firstly a gift to yourself. Everyone is special. As you make the charm, it, too, becomes special. It represents your current thoughts and feelings, and when you give your love charm, you pass on that respect and uniqueness. Giving a love charm is a sign that you truly honour and love that person.

LEFT: *Love charms can be made from everyday objects you see around you or you can gather together a collection with a charm in mind.*

OPPOSITE: Romeo and Juliet, *1884 by Sir Frank Dicksee (1853–1928). A beautiful painting of one of the most potent love stories ever told.*

Love is patient and kind; love is not jealous or boastful; it is not arrogant or rude. Love does not insist on its own way; it is not irritable or resentful; it does not rejoice at wrong, but rejoices in the right. Love bears all things, believes all things, hopes all things, endures all things.

1 Corinthians, 13 (4–7)

The Art of Giving

To give without expectation is the essence of a love charm. When you give expecting something in return, you do not love wholeheartedly, you love conditionally.

Giving a love charm as a bargain for gratitude, forgiveness or promises is an act of egoism, not of the true self. You are dishonouring yourself, the person to whom you are giving the gift and your relationship.

The joy of giving is never to want anything in return. Making a love charm is an act of unconditional expression. You are creating something that may have the briefest of existences; it may be given and forgotten or it may be treasured for a lifetime. It does not matter which and does not change how valuable the charm is or the intent with which it was made.

The Way to Give

A truthful person should not judge how a person receives a gift. In giving, you speak the truth of your heart and show the recipient your deepest love and honour. You may feel he or she has not heard, may not care, or may not even understand. This is the voice of your ego judging that person's response. In judging another person you show that you no longer trust or believe in him or her.

The making and giving of a love charm must be done with the whole self, which is who you are when you are not dwelling on the past or the future. You must live in each heartbeat, accepting every moment with pleasure.

LEFT: *Flowers have long been a token of love and affection and are given not only to lovers, but friends and family.* Tristan and Isolde, *1904 by Andrew Watson Turnball.*

"Yesterday's the past and tomorrow's the future. Today is a gift, which is why they call it the present."

Bill Keane

The Art of Receiving

When someone honours you with a gift, he or she reminds you that you are special, that you are unique in this world. You should return that honour and accept the gift with an open heart.

The ego may say that you are not worthy or that you are too proud, but your true self feels the love inherent in the gift and will shine through, if you let it. The gift may be a compliment, a present, a touch or a simple glance. These gifts are offered to your heart so you should let it speak openly in reply.

You should give without expectation or judgement and you should receive gifts in this way. If you are responding honestly, without wanting something in return, then you do not have anything to fear. If you do not judge the gift, whether it is bought or handmade, whether it is large or small, then you see only the intent behind it. All gifts are equal. The difference is in how you perceive them.

Accepting Gifts

A gift is a beautiful thing and should be received with beauty and grace. A love charm captures the beauty in your heart. If you accept a love charm with the deepest honour and respect, so you honour and respect the giver.

Receiving is an art that has been lost to many; people sometimes feel self-conscious when someone pays a compliment, or can be suspicious of an invitation. They often choose to see only the shadows of a person's motives. The cynical voice inside the head drowns out the innocence of the heart. A world full of shadows is a dark place. Let go of your fears and accept with wisdom and not question the intent behind a person's gift. Look for only the light of his or her heart's intentions.

You are given each day as something new to experience. All you must do is accept it for the gift that it is. Gifts also come from people's hearts and fill your everyday life, whether they be simple words, a touch or the offer of food. It is up to you to accept these things and see them for what they truly are, a love charm for your own unique heart.

LEFT: *Gifts do not have to be of material value: gestures and kindnesses are of great value.* The Kiss *by Sir Lawrence Alma-Tadema (1836–1912).*

Legendary Love Charms

Tales of love charms are woven into the myths and legends of every culture, and show how a spell, song, sacred object or creature strengthens the connection between two people to draw them closer together.

In Celtic mythology, the hero, Diarmuid, had a beauty spot on his cheek which enticed Gráinne, the wife of his chief to run away with him. He refused her love until she put a *geasa*, a word of power on him, and he became her lover. The *geasa* is a love charm, a simple word, which if spoken from the heart can give birth to something new and passionate. Words can have the power to bring love to life.

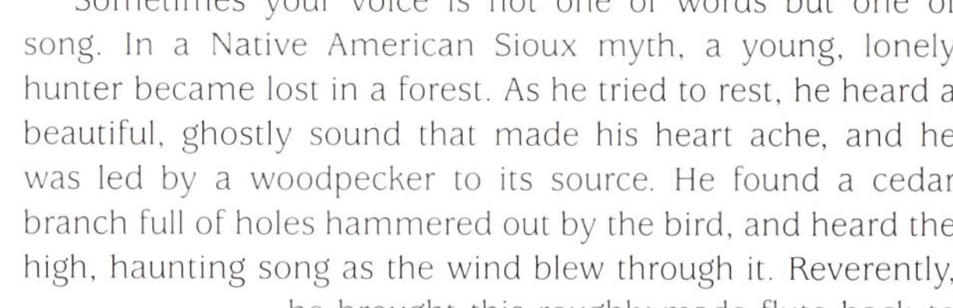

Sometimes your voice is not one of words but one of song. In a Native American Sioux myth, a young, lonely hunter became lost in a forest. As he tried to rest, he heard a beautiful, ghostly sound that made his heart ache, and he was led by a woodpecker to its source. He found a cedar branch full of holes hammered out by the bird, and heard the high, haunting song as the wind blew through it. Reverently, he brought this roughly-made flute back to his people and composed a special song for his *winchinchala*, his sweetheart. Its beautiful sound transfixed her, bringing her to him and she agreed to marry him. The Sioux regard the flute as an instrument for speaking to the heart of a loved one.

Love charms can also symbolize the eternal and spiritual nature of love. According to legend, Tristan, nephew of King Mark of Cornwall, and Iseult, Mark's future Queen, mistakenly drank a love potion intended for the King. They fell deeply in love and for a time the lovers met in secret. The King discovered their affair and Tristan left for voluntary exile in Brittany. Eventually the tragic pair were buried side by side and, above their graves, two yew trees grew so close together that they became entwined. Yew trees regenerate and in many religions they are thought to aid the passing of a soul from death into a new life. Love, like the yew tree, is also part of an eternal cycle of birth, death and rebirth, and only by accepting that cycle will you be able to love forever.

In Greek mythology, the goddess of love, beauty and fertility, Aphrodite, often used

the ugliest man alive. But Cupid fell in love with Psyche and hid her in a secret place where he could visit her every night. He told her never to try to see his face, but one night she lit a lamp and saw Cupid beside her. He reproached her and fled, fearing what his mother might do to him now that his secret was discovered. Psyche searched the world for Cupid, until the god Jupiter granted her immortality and gave her in marriage to Cupid.

Love charms have as much potential to do harm as to do good; what goes around, comes around. You should be willing to receive similar vibes to the one's you generate.

OPPOSITE: Tristran and Iseult Drinking the Love Potion, *1867 by Dante Gabriel Rossetti (1828–82).*

LEFT: The Mirror of Venus, *c. 1885 by Edward Burne-Jones.*

BELOW: Cupid Delivering Psyche, *1867 by Edward Burne-Jones (1833–98).*

spells and charms to do her mischievous work on the gods and mortals alike. She is an iconic figure, born from the foam of the sea and is often depicted rising from the waves. Her charms often had poor consequences, as she frequently seduced men and exerted her heavenly powers to satisfy her own erotic pleasure, and not her heart. She was said to charm the god of war, Ares, into her bed, but was caught by her husband, Hephaistos. Zeus, the ruler of the gods, punished her infidelity by forcing her to sleep with a mortal.

Cupid was the Roman god of love and the son of Venus, the Roman goddess of love. He was often depicted as a cherubic, but capricious and wanton boy, armed with a quiver full of "arrowed desires" or a torch to inflame love in the hearts of gods and men. Some of his arrows, however, would turn people away from those who fell in love with them.

According to one myth, Venus was jealous of the beautiful mortal, Psyche (Greek for "soul") and told Cupid to make her love

FAIRYTALE LOVE CHARMS

THE WORLD IS RICH IN ALLEGORICAL FAIRYTALES THAT SPEAK OF THE CONNECTION A LOVE CHARM CAN BRING TO TWO PEOPLE.

In the tale of *Beauty and the Beast*, it was the charm or gift of a rose that brought the two lovers together. A man picked the rose for his daughter, Beauty, but the beast, who owned the rose bush, demanded her life in exchange for the gift. Beauty agreed to live with the beast in his castle and in time came to care for him. One day, she left to see her father, but the beast began to die without her. She rushed back and declared her love for him and in so doing released him from a spell and he became a prince. The rose brought the two lovers together, but it was the words of Beauty that transformed their love and brought it to life.

This act of declaring love, of giving wholeheartedly, is so magical and powerful that fairytales abound with it. The frog-prince was transformed by the kiss of a princess. In the story of *Sleeping Beauty*, she was woken by the kiss of a prince, as she lay surrounded by enchanted rose thorns. By expressing what is in their hearts, everybody has the capability to transform someone else.

The story of Cinderella has many roots. One of them, Grimm's *Aschenputtel*, is a story of how a love charm can motivate someone to fulfil a heart's dream. Aschenputtel planted a hazel twig on her mother's grave. A tree grew and a

dove came to nest there. One day a prince invited her ugly stepsisters and her to three balls. On the first night, she was left behind and she sat under the tree in despair. The dove heard her crying and it fetched her a dress as a gift to wear to the ball. She went to each ball and danced with the prince.

After the third ball, in her rush to get home, she left a slipper behind. The prince visited every house looking for her. Finally he was united with Aschenputtel. The dove was the charm that spoke to her and acted to bring their love together. But it was only because she was looking for love that the dove's message was heard.

A love charm may sound in the smallest moments; you should always try to listen for its call.

The fairytale of Rapunzel tells of how love can heal the deepest wounds. A witch locked Rapunzel in a high tower, but she was visited by a prince who climbed up her long hair to her window. One day, the witch found them together and threw the prince from the window. He fell on to a patch of thorns and was blinded. The witch sent Rapunzel to a land far away. Years later, the prince, who had been blindly wandering, heard her singing, and they were reunited. Rapunzel's tears of joy cascaded into the prince's eyes, healing his lost vision.

OPPOSITE TOP: *From* Beauty and the Beast *by Edmund Dulac (1882–1953).*

OPPOSITE BOTTOM: The Sleeping Beauty *by Thomas Ralph Spence (1855–1918).*

RIGHT: Rapunzel, *1908 by Frank Cadogan Cowper (1877–1958).*

Courting Charms

Many ancient traditions for the giving of love charms have been passed down over the years and still survive today. Some are rituals for courting and marriage; others are part of the timeless quest for a faithful, loving partner.

Whether by insight or by searching, innumerable love charms and rites have always been used to find a true partner and love. Food is especially symbolic in all parts of the world. Fruit, as a rich fertility symbol, has been used often in courting rituals. Many foods have a meaning – it might come from their shape, colour, taste or history. Apples have long been symbolic of love and fertility.

Giving food and the act of cooking for someone you love can be a charm or means of seduction. Baking a cake or cooking a delicious symbolic meal for a person you love is as important today as it was hundreds of years ago.

Wedding cakes have been a symbol of love for centuries and sharing the cake is significant of sharing love. Trees and plants also receive symbolic meaning. Their leaves, the places they grow, the way their branches reach to the sky, can all have some relevance to your lives and love if you see it. Trees led to one of the first ancient alphabets and wood rituals have been used for love charms all over the world. Flowers, too, have a long history as lover's gifts. A "language" of flowers has become popular, and lovers still give flowers on special days.

Tea

As part of the elaborate Chinese courting ritual the man would give the woman and her family *cha-li*, or tea presents. Tea, along with other gifts, such as sugar, wine, tobacco, cake and poultry, was presented and distributed by strict etiquette. Making tea for someone is a common ritual today, but even simple rituals can be important when imparting love.

LEFT: *An intimate meal with the person you love can be a part of a love charming ritual.*

Apple Pips

An apple was once cut in half and the pips counted. An even number of pips would indicate that a new love would lead to a happy marriage. An odd number was a sign that the woman would remain unmarried for some time. If a pip had been cut through, then the love would be stormy and ultimately faithless, if two pips had been cut then the love was doomed to fade.

Beech Bark

Beech bark was the first paper used for writing magical inscriptions. If you found some beech bark or wood, you could use it as part of an ancient wishing spell whereby you would inscribe your wish upon the bark and bury it in the ground. As the bark was consumed by the earth, so the wish would be released into the world and it would begin to show itself in your life.

Hazelnuts

The hazel was believed to be a tree of knowledge and wisdom. Hazelnuts were revered as the food of gods. At Hallowe'en, a lover could take two hazelnuts, one for each person, and throw them into a fire. If they lay there quietly side by side, the match was deemed faithful, but if one nut moved away from the other, it was believed that one of the pair was unfaithful at heart.

Birch Garland

Birch is a tree symbolizing the birth of something new. In pagan times, silver birch was especially revered as a tree of feminine creation and wisdom. A Welsh ritual called for a man to weave a garland of birch wood and leaves and give it to the woman he loved. If she reciprocated his feelings, she would return the favour and present him with a garland. The garlands were a pledge of their love.

Marriage Charms

There are many different marriage charms and gifts exchanged between men and women across the world to symbolize commitment. The tradition of giving tokens of love to one another in a marriage ritual has existed for centuries and the objects exchanged are deeply significant.

Rings

The giving of a ring to symbolize a marriage bond derives from the Anglo-Saxon ceremony where a woman transferred her lands to a house-man, or husband. The man would hand the woman a ring along with his wealth and declare that he would worship and honour her. The wife would then accept the ring, as a token of their eternal union, and agree to the familiar vows, including the now unused phrase, "to be bonny and buxom in bed". The marriage ceremonies of many cultures include the giving or exchange of rings and other items of jewellery, but the type of wedding ring and finger on which it is worn varies.

Lock of Hair

Hair is a deeply personal and expressive part of your body. Ownership of a person's hair was considered to impart a magic bond between two people. In Ireland, a man would offer a woman he loved a woven bracelet of hair, which, if she accepted, symbolized their permanent connection. In more recent times a lock of a lover's hair, curled into a circle, would be kept in a love locket. The circle of hair, like the woven hair bracelet, indicated a love that was eternal and timeless. This attitude sentimentally manifested itself in the custom of a widow's mourning jewellery made from the hair of her dead husband.

Jumping the Broomstick

The custom of jumping the broomstick goes back many hundreds of years. A man and woman would take each other's hands in front of a witness, their grasp forming the symbol of eternity. They were said to be handfasted, married for a year and a day. The couple then jumped over a broomstick made of birch twigs. The birch symbolized the letting go of the past and the bringing in of the new.

This was considered "common-law" marriage and was a popular marriage custom in Britain until, in the 16th century, the Church legalized marriage ceremonies, but only those conducted by a priest.

Decorated Squash

In the Slavic region, a man wanting to propose properly to a woman would present her with an earthenware pot containing squash. The pot was a sign of permanence and would be displayed over her hearth, should she welcome his courtship. The squash were symbols of love and fertility. Each squash was decorated with polished stones, a work of craftsmanship performed by the man for his love. If the woman consented to be his wife, the stones would become part of a wedding anklet, which was the symbol of her status as a married woman. This elaborate decoration of food is a powerful love charm.

Tokens for Love Charms

There are many symbols and objects that can be used when making love charms. Symbols of the earth include trees, animals, flowers and stones, while symbols of the soul include words and letters, patterns and pictures, and body and motion.

Trees

The language of trees, their unique characteristics and symbolism, have always been a part of charms and ceremonies. By walking through a forest and noticing how each tree is different, you can find something that speaks to your heart personally. The wood, bark, leaves or fruit of a tree can be used in creating an individual love charm.

Love Ritual

Find a space outdoors where you feel at peace with yourself. Look at any trees around you. Notice how unique each one is. See if a tree catches your attention and gather a fallen branch or twig from it. Use the branch as a talisman to remind you of the tree and that special place.

Apple Tree

The apple tree is a symbol of love and peace. Offering an apple or apple blossom is a display of timeless love. The Norse goddess, Iduna, and the Greek god, Apollo, both protected an apple tree laden with the golden fruit of immortality and youth. Apple wood can be carved into amulets and talismans for love and longevity. Apple blossom was scattered to mark a place as sacred to love.

Willow Tree

The willow bends easily to the wind; it is a tree of forgiveness and acceptance, of balance and flexibility. You need all of these as you walk the path of a loving relationship. Willow is a great healer; its bark contains the same ingredients of aspirin. Willow often grows by rivers and streams; water cleanses you, washes off the past and helps to heal old wounds.

Holly Tree

The holly is a guardian tree. Its sharp, spiky leaves protect its red berries. Mistletoe is often found growing close to holly in mid-winter and the two plants together symbolize male and female fertility. Weaving a garland of holly and mistletoe is still a custom at Yuletide today, allowing the male and female to become entangled in an unbroken circle.

Flowers

These are beautiful and transitory. They are a symbol of opening, awakening and passion. Through its colour, a flower calls out to be pollinated, to join with its fertile partner. We give flowers to call out to one another, to speak our hearts to people. Oils from flowers, such as camomile, jasmine and lavender, can be used for wonderful aromatic love charms. Aromatherapy massages, baths and perfumes can be a simple, direct expression of the heart.

Love Ritual

Take the time to smell the scent of the flowers around you. Notice what each scent brings to mind: a memory or a sensation. Find a scent that reminds you of something joyful, and place a bunch of those flowers somewhere special in your home.

Rose

This is a timeless symbol of love and regeneration. The first red rose was supposed to come from the blood of Aphrodite, the Greek goddess of love, who trod on a white rose and bled. Death symbolized by a white rose can lead to new life and love (the red rose). The thorns of the rose and its blood-red colour are reminders of the pain of being reborn. Letting go of the past is a difficult but necessary part of opening the heart to the possibility of new love to come. The rose can be a token of accepting love unconditionally.

Lily

The lily gives off a pungent perfume that can stimulate the heart. The white flowers are symbolic of purity, peace and innocence. It was said that lilies grew up where drops of milk from the earth goddess, Hera, fell to the ground when she created the Milky Way. The lily was sacred to the ancient eastern goddess, Astarte, symbolizing the rebirth of love and life at that time of year. The lily can bring a return to innocence and peace after a storm. It is a reminder that mistakes offer a chance to learn and be renewed.

ABOVE: *Roses and other flowers have been the gifts of lovers for thousands of years.*

Animals

The animal kingdom was considered to be wise and a source of guidance and understanding. An animal can touch our spirits. Particular animals may already have meaning for you, for example, a bird that is nesting nearby or the memory of a dolphin at sea. What you feel and associate with those moments can help you find what you are looking for.

Love Ritual

Notice what animals or insects are living close to you. Is there one that you see often nearby?

Watch the way it moves. Listen to hear if it has a song.

See if there is something that uplifts you and share that feeling with someone you love.

Dove

The dove is not only an image of peace and love, but also of rebirth. Dove feathers can be used in love charms. The gypsy people believed that the dove represented woman and the serpent represented man, and that together they brought new life. The dove was sacred to Aphrodite in her role as a bringer of death and new love, and it was a dove that told Noah that new life could begin after the Great Flood.

Seal

These abound in Celtic mythology, such as the Selkie who came ashore on certain nights and shed their skins to become beautiful women until they returned to the ocean at dawn. They are symbols of change, of the wisdom that comes from within, and reminders that to live with love and beauty you must accept and celebrate that the person you love, as well as you, will constantly change.

Swan

The white swan is a divine bird, closely associated with purity, love and amorousness. The fierce Norse Valkyries wore magical, swan-feather cloaks during their rides from Valhalla. Brahma and Zeus were reincarnated into a swan to give birth to the world. The swan is a symbol of transformation. By accepting the transformation of love you can accept and respond to its passion.

Stones

Rocks and stones are formed under great stress and earthly forces. Each stone on a beach is different; some appear to have faces or animals staring out from them. Giving a stone as a love charm is an ancient ritual. A stone from your garden can be as special as one set in an engagement ring.

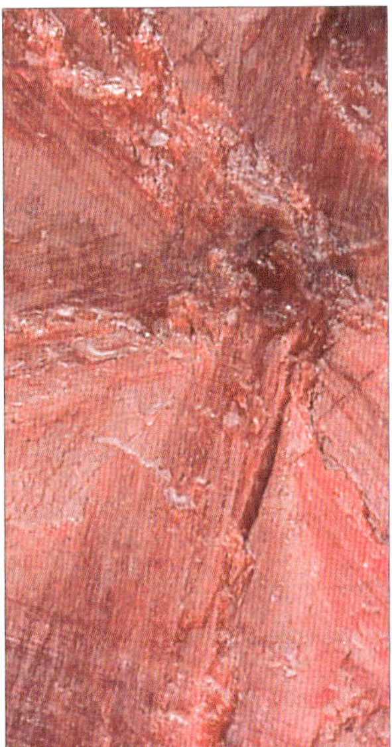

Love Ritual

Go for a walk and look at the stones that you pass, whether they are on a gravel path, in a wall or on a beach. See if you can notice a face on the stone. If you see one, think of whose face it reminds you of. Pick it up, if you can, and give it to the person you love. Tell him or her what it means to you.

Diamond

Literally translated from Latin, diamond means world goddess. It is the hardest mineral substance known on Earth and was said to rule all other stones. In Tibet, the World Goddess was reincarnated as a diamond and this association with a virgin goddess developed into its symbolism as a new beginning. It is also a symbol of indestructible love.

Ruby

The ruby's rich deep-red, rose, carmine or even purple colour symbolizes vitality and passionate love. Its richness was thought to overcome illness and disease by cleansing the wearer of negative emotions and feelings. The ruby is a stone of passion, raising feelings and thoughts from fear and sadness to love and joy.

Pearl

The shimmering pearl and its spherical shape is associated with the cycle of the moon and with the circle of eternity. It was believed that a pearl was formed when lightning struck the eye of a shellfish. Lightning is a powerful symbol of wisdom from the sky, and pearls are a sign of knowledge and understanding. It is also a symbol of perfection.

Cut or uncut rubies when used in love charms are symbols of passion.

Words and Letters

Writing or carving symbols and words was considered sacred and extremely powerful by many old cultures. When you hold a word or symbol in your mind and commit that permanently into the world by transcribing it, you are transferring your thoughts into reality. Inscribing a special mark, word or phrase into an object can help you to communicate your dreams to the world and, by destroying that object, allow you to let go of past dreams.

Love Ritual

Think of a phrase, a line in a poem or a saying that has some personal meaning for you. Take the first letter of each word and spend some time arranging them on a page. Create a pattern with the letters, perhaps linking them in a circle.

This inscription on this bindrune means "to gain inspiration".

Runes

The Norse runic alphabet has many letters which can be combined together to create a single symbol. Each letter had some deep significance, which was used for divination as much as writing. For example, *Ansuz*, or mouth, is the letter for speaking and communicating. *Gyfu* is the letter for giving: its cross shape symbolizes the connection between two people. *Beorc* is the rune for new beginnings. Other runes that may be useful in creating a love charm are given in the Table of Symbols.

Inscription

Inscribing words or a phrase, or even just a date, on to an object is a wonderful way to endow that object with memories and dreams. It has always been common for jewellery, when given as a gift, to be inscribed with secret words or a poem which would be understood only by the wearer. Any gift can be made unique by writing, carving, painting, or stitching on it some words of special meaning. The words can transform any object into a symbol of love.

Monogram

Taking the initials of two people's names and drawing those letters entwined together symbolizes their union. Spend some time designing a monogram for your relationship. Let your feelings express themselves freely in the contours of the letters. Consider all the unique ways in which your two lives overlap and shape those into the monogram. Creating something that uniquely defines your relationship is a symbol of your active intent to entwine your two lives together.

Patterns and Pictures

The image and its associated meaning contained within a picture or pattern can sometimes communicate something deep inside you. A landscape from a holiday, a sunset on a beach, or the wings of a butterfly can all have deep significance. Pictures have been used to express feelings throughout history. Giving a picture as a symbol of the journey you are sharing with someone is a profound way of honouring your path together.

Love Ritual

Find several objects that are important to you. Arrange them together in any way under a light or in the sun and then look at the shadows that they make. Draw the outline of a part of the shadow to make a pattern. This pattern is a symbol of all the meanings of those special objects.

Shapes

The outline of a shape, the number of its sides and its colour can have special significance if you choose. The perfect symmetry of a circle is a timeless symbol of eternity. The crescent moon and its thirteen phases is a symbol of balance: light against dark, reminding us that all things wax and wane naturally. The three sides and points of a triangle represent the three aspects to life and a living relationship – youth, maturity and learned wisdom. The five-pointed star speaks of brightness and passion. The square is a symbol of equality and strength.

Knots

The Celts used a sacred love knot to tie two people together. It was said to cast a spell over the lovers until the knot was untied. The intricate designs of the Celtic knot are never-ending lines, symbolizing the eternal nature of life and love. The Celts often used animals in imagery, their mouths holding their tails, creating a design of writhing creatures. Weaving a pattern using two threads is a sign of sharing your path with someone. Folktales from all over the world tell of how a woman seeks to bind her lover by tying knots in a possession, such as a riding whip or girdle.

A Celtic triple spiral symbolizing love, marriage and birth has a never-ending quality.

Body and Motion

The way you move your body speaks more intuitively and honestly of your actions, thoughts and feelings than any symbol. Your touch, the way you smile and the rhythm of your dance are the truest symbols of your feelings. Your body is a doorway through which you express your soul, your fears, your hopes and your love.

Love Ritual

When you are with someone you care about, ask him or her if they would like a hug. If he or she accepts, hug him or her with your heart beating against one another's. In those moments, think about how you feel about that person and try to let your body express those thoughts. A hug is a wonderful gift of joy, compassion and love.

Music and rhythm have made people dance and express their feelings since the earliest times.

Dance

When you move your body in time and in step with the person you love, you are communicating on the deepest level. Many cultures see dance as the doorway to wisdom and knowledge. If you let go and give yourself to the dance, if you forget about performing in front of other people or behaving for someone else and let every muscle respond, you are letting your body naturally call out to your soulmate. Your soulmate is a person who can understand your dance and the expression of your body, and respond to you intuitively.

Touch

The magical gift of touch, the sensation of another body pressing its warmth against your own, is profound. The touch of a person's hand can open something deep inside you. Often, the touch of another can help you to release something. Touching someone can be both healing and sensual, such as when giving a massage. Touch offers comfort and reminds you that you are not alone – it can make you feel wanted, needed and that you are part of the world – whether a tribe, a culture, or a family – and always a part of the Earth.

Seasons and Cycles

Different times of the year had huge symbolism for couples in the past. Each season was linked to life shared with the land. Even today, our bodies respond to the light and the temperature outside, so that we tend to be reflective by the fire in winter and active in the sun in summer. Other cycles are equally important, such as a woman's menstrual cycle, which ebbs and flows with the moon. Choosing a time to give a love charm within these cycles can give it another level of significance.

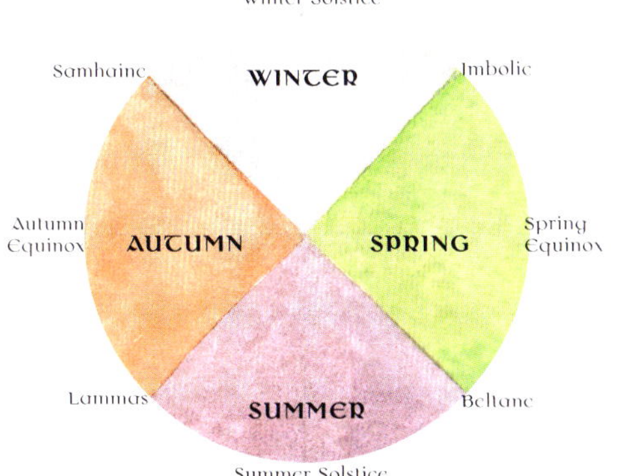

The thirteen stages of the moon, from no moon to full moon.

Wheel of the Year

The Celts believed that all things begin in darkness, in winter, which is a time for letting go of the old and welcoming in the new. It is a time of accepting the past, a time of forgiveness and a time for wounds to be healed. In winter, you dream of the year to come. Spring comes with the leaves. It is the season of awakening and preparation and when you express the dreams of winter. May Day, at the end of spring, was the traditional day to be married. In summer and the time of passion, you reap what you have sown in spring. Then, during the embers of autumn you reach a peace with all those around you, become fulfilled and let go of the dreams of the past to begin the cycle again as winter approaches once more.

Thirteen Moons

A woman's menstrual cycle has always been closely connected with the waxing and waning of the moon. It takes 13 nights for the moon to grow from new to full, which gave the number 13 its auspicious reputation, and the full 26 days is the length of a menstrual cycle. At the full moon, a woman is often ovulating and at her most fertile; this is a time of new beginnings when her body might become filled with life. The new moon, the dark moon, was considered by the Celts a time of death and rebirth; it was often when a woman would withdraw to begin menstruating during her "moon time". This is a time of powerful initiation, wisdom and learning. In many cultures the moon goddess protects lovers.

Love Ritual

During the morning, write down your dreams for the day ahead; perhaps these are things you would like to share with someone you love. Put it to one side. In the evening, read your list of dreams and remember those that you made come true during the day and those that never happened. Forget about all of them, let them go, and focus on the moment you have there and then.

THE CYCLE OF LOVE

The art of giving a love charm is that of listening, both to yourself and to the person you are giving to. You must always be aware of the intent with which you are filling the charm, so that you are always giving from the deepest part of your heart and not from the demands of your ego.

The word charm stems from the Latin word for spell or song, *carmen*. The Roman goddess, Carmenta was known for her words of power and was credited with adapting the Greek alphabet for use with Latin.

A charm was a song or incantation sung by a woman to exert her power, the power of words and love, over a man. Love songs and ballads remain extremely popular and are still sung to give messages of love to someone special. To charm your lover was to spellbind him and cause him to feel lovesick and to act more passionately. Love charms were associated with enchantment and the weaving of love between two people. To give a love charm is the art of expressing yourself towards another, to charm him. Love charms are also an opportunity for you to express the changes and challenges that you face in love. It is a chance for you to look more closely within yourself for an answer to the problems that may lie before you and present them to the person we love. In a bustling world, love charms are a symbol of gentler thoughts and a reminder of feelings that you may have forgotten to show in your life and to the people around you.

Love has always been considered an act of nature, a source of irrational behaviour, as when people feel irrevocably drawn together or suffer love sickness. Just think of some of the common expressions of irrationality that people use: to be mad about someone, blindly in love, thinks the world of, love to distraction, swept off one's feet, and even worships the ground he or she walks on.

These feelings are all part of a cycle of love, around which you are drawn. Love can open you up to new possibilities and new dreams. You are always changed by its touch on your life.

ABOVE: *Relationships can be in constant state of flux. By communicating your feelings and remaining close, you can adapt to changes.*

Wheel of Love

Love is always in Motion It is always changing and you are drawn around its cycle of growing and learning. To love deeply is to accept that each moment you share in love is transitory, and that the next will bring something new. Love charms can help you flow around that cycle, help you give and forgive, love and be loved.

Love is a natural part of the world and, as with the Wheel of the Year, you can think of the Cycle of Love as a wheel with four seasons.

The Season of Dreams is the start, the time when you are alone or feeling disconnected from your life. This is the time you focus on the dreams of love to come and what needs to change to bring that about. Then, as love begins to flourish and open again, you enter the Season of Hope, the hope that your dreams are being fulfilled. This is the time of innocence and gentleness, moving slowly and carefully as your love deepens. Next comes the Season of Passion. Now you have opened yourself out completely to the other person and feel safe to express your love from every pore of your body. When passion peaks and balances and you find that new possibilities have opened up and that you have been changed by your love, this is the Season of Fulfilment. Now is the time that love heals and renews you until you find you must let go of your old dreams and begin to dream again.

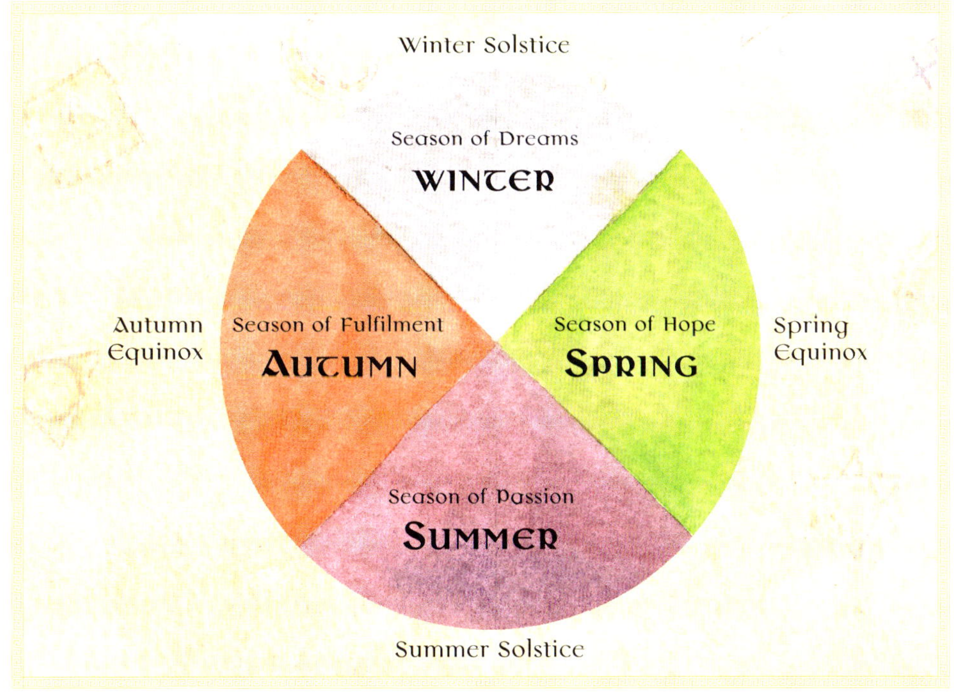

Season of Dreams

This is a time of beginnings, when you pause for a moment and consider where you want to be going and where you have been. What were your dreams? What are your dreams now?

This can be a time when you are alone, or a time when you realize that love has changed you. It is time to reassess your relationships and yourself.

In the Season of Dreams it is dark and you may feel frightened, angry or impatient for something brighter and better to come along. However, in the darkness, you have an opportunity to imagine something completely new and different, to branch out in a new direction. Dreams are your guide – you can map them, follow them and they will lead you to the inner voice of your heart.

This is often a season of frustration, when you find that life is a little harder on you. You must find space in your life for yourself, get to know what makes you happy, what makes you sad, the daydreams you have, and the nightmares. All these dreams are voices from your heart telling you what you want next and what must heal before you can take the steps towards your goal.

It is a time for taking stock of the lessons learned, using them to guide you in what you need next in life, whether it is a new love or the rekindling and transformation of an old love.

As with winter, it is a period of stillness and of waiting and of listening. This is a good time to be alone, even for just a short while, to notice how you feel in your life and your heart. Love charms, as a path for finding your true inner self which may have become muffled in the day-to-day of your life, or drowned in recent pain, will help you. These quiet, contemplative love charms are tokens of the dreams that you are forming for the future and for what has happened in the past that you must now relinquish.

LEFT: *In the Season of Dreams, as with winter, it is a good time to take stock, think and prepare for the coming regeneration of spring.*

OPPOSITE: *Look inwards and examine your relationships.*

Dreams take you on a journey through your consciousness and desires, and help you discover what you need in your life to find love and happiness. Your dreams are the calling of your heart.

Preparation

During the Season of Dreams you need to focus on your own needs and dreams, since you cannot make another person happy without being happy yourself.

Keep a notepad by your bed and write down any dreams you remember. Think about what they mean to you and what feelings they evoke. If they are dreams of seeking out something, think about what you were seeking. If it was a nightmare, were you being chased, and if so, by what and why did it make you afraid?

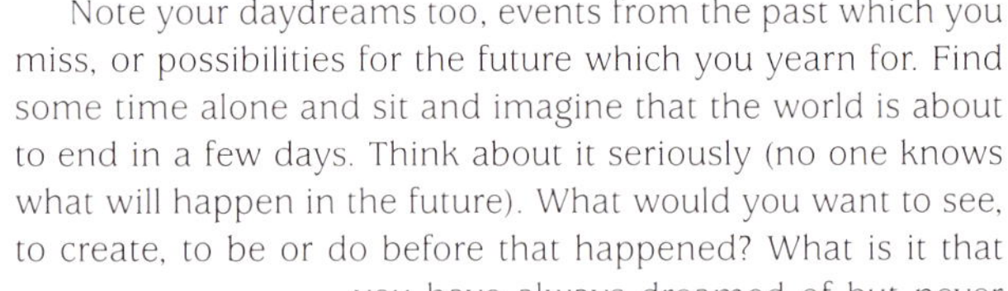

Note your daydreams too, events from the past which you miss, or possibilities for the future which you yearn for. Find some time alone and sit and imagine that the world is about to end in a few days. Think about it seriously (no one knows what will happen in the future). What would you want to see, to create, to be or do before that happened? What is it that you have always dreamed of but never been able to do? What are the unspoken dreams you carry with you? If they are simple, or even if they seem impossible, write them down.

Now gather up all those dreams and feelings and think. Which are the most important to you? Which ones make your heart beat faster? Which ones would make you feel happy? Which ones would you want to share with someone you love? Which ones would you want to do alone?

All these dreams could be possibilities that you can make happen. Each one could become true if you want it to; it is only a matter of accepting the consequences each might bring and learning from the mistakes along the way. Everyone possesses the power to make changes in their lives and, by imagining their dreams, they take that small step towards being truly happy within themselves.

These are your dreams for the coming cycle.

LEFT: *Try to remember your dreams on waking and think of what they mean. Keeping a notebook by the bed reminds you to write them down while they are fresh in your mind.*

Meditation

This meditation is for clearing the mind of day-to-day worries, allowing you to focus on your inner voice. Once you can quieten your mind, you can easily notice the dreams and needs of your heart and express them in a charm. This may take some practice and you may be surprised at how loud and busy your mind is. Once you master this, do it with your eyes open, so that you can clear your mind, no matter what the distraction.

1 Sit cross-legged with your back straight, head up and your hands clasped and relaxed in front of you. It should not feel too comfortable. Start with your eyes closed. Notice the thoughts in your mind, the background noise, the sounds and smells around you. Now, as each thought comes into your mind, let it go again, do not dwell on anything. Let your thoughts become tranquil and your mind empty.

2 Breathe in slowly and count your first breath. Do not let your mind wander, focus on your body and the moment. Breathe out slowly. Count ten slow breaths like this, just being and breathing in the moment with no thought of the past or future. Let yourself focus totally on the present; allow the clutter of your mind fade into silence.

Dream Catcher Love Charm

A dream catcher is a Native American charm for capturing good, wise dreams and for letting bad dreams pass through and away into the night. This is a love charm for awakening the dreams both you and the person you love hold inside your hearts.

Traditionally, a dream catcher is hung above a sleeping person's head, to keep wise dreams so that they can be remembered on waking and so that bad dreams can be forgotten. When you give your love charm, offer to help him or her hang it up and explain your intentions behind the gift. You could also spend some time listening to his or her dreams and sharing your own with your love.

If this is a time of calling love into your life, hang the dream catcher above your bed and listen to your dreams.

Spend a moment considering the wood or tree you want to use for the dream catcher. Also think about what colour ribbon and wool (yarn) you feel would be most appropriate in the charm. Gather feathers that come across your path on a walk or at home, for example.

The dream catcher has a single thread that is wound in a spiral from the outside to the centre, symbolizing the journey from the waking world to the world of dreams. The Native Americans believe that their dreaming selves pass through the heart of a dream catcher and return with knowledge of the dreams of their true selves.

You will need

- Fallen branch
- Knife
- Ball of coloured wool (yarn)
- Ribbon
- Feathers

LEFT: *The dream catcher is a charm to call in all the deepest dreams and desires of one's heart. It is a gift symbolizing the awakening of a person's heart and your willingness to follow his or her dream.*

1 Find a long, flexible branch from the place you choose and bend it into a circle. You may find you need to trim nodules and smooth the bark.

2 Slice across the branch at both ends so that they lie flat against each other. Secure the ends together using coloured wool (yarn).

3 Cover the circle with ribbon and fasten it securely at one end. This forms the simple outer loop of the dream catcher.

4 Tie the wool to the circle and wind it around the circle a few centimetres (inches) away, not too tautly. Repeat at equal distances around the circle. This is the spiral of thread that weaves into the centre.

5 When you have almost completed the circle, wind the wool around the centre of the next wool span. Repeat this spiral structure until you have a small central circle and then tie off the wool end.

6 Use the wool to secure feathers to your charm. They can be tied either to the branch so that they hang down from the dream catcher, or secured to a wool span, perhaps at the centre. Think about the person this is intended for and follow your instincts.

Dream Space Love Charm

This is a charm that creates a special place for love to rest. It is a place that reminds someone of all the wonderful dreams that love has and will fulfil.

At this time, in the season of dreams, you need to remember what has happened in your life, good and bad, and create new dreams to share with someone. A dream space is a shrine to the past and is also dedicated to the future of a relationship. It is a physical space that you give over to your dreams, as a step towards your dreams physically manifesting themselves in your life. Think carefully about hte place where you want to create the dream space. It should be somewhere you share with the person you love, perhaps even a place outdoors.

Present the dream space love charm and all its intentions to the person you love. Light a candle with him or her in front of the pattern you have created. Spend some time thinking and talking about those dreams. Think about what steps you might have to take to make them come true. Whenever you feel the need, come back to the dream space, light the candle and recall your dream. Remember the steps you must take to get there and how far along the path you have come.

You will need

Picture of a special place or person
Stones
Any other special items from a relationship (such as jewellery)
Candles

1 Find a picture that signifies something both of you dream of, something you want to share together in the future, such as a place you want to travel to or a person you want to see. Think of dreams you have already shared together, and any special items you already have from those dreams. Gather some stones from a special place and focus on the future you want to create with that person.

2 Place the stones around the picture in a shape or pattern that you feel represents your dreams. This may be a circle representing the eternal bond you share, or perhaps a star for the passion that you feel needs to enter into your life. Choose whatever shape feels right for you. Experiment with the pattern until it feels right. Add your other special items.

3 If you have a special item that links with the picture, you could place it above or below the picture, if you wish. Spend time focusing where you want the picture.

4 Place the candles around the space, arranging them in a way you feel is appropriate. Remember never to leave burning candles unattended.

Season of Hope

In the Season of Hope new love is beginning to blossom. In the Season of Dreams you demonstrated your intention for change in your life and now something has been kindled, or resurrected, or it has simply altered its course towards your dream. It is a gentle time, where you must be patient and let the love grow slowly and delicately. It is not a time to rush into things but to realize the beauty and wonder of the love that has entered into your life.

During the Season of Hope you may be treasure-hunting – listening and watching for the signs in yourself and in others that love is entering your life. You must turn over every rock, watch for every clue that may lead you to your heart's desire. The world is beckoning you onwards to fulfil your dreams; remain alert to heed its call. Be persistent, be joyful in your search; everything comes to those who wait. Soon, love will appear quietly and completely, enveloping your life.

Now you can begin to touch, smell and taste love around you; it fills your senses. Now is the time to respond to it with all your heart, openly without cynicism, without idealizing it, remembering that it, too, is transitory and will change.

What you do in the Season of Hope is the first step towards realizing the dreams that you experienced in the time before. You must keep in mind where you want to be and celebrate the first uncertain steps without getting waylaid on your journey by the heady feelings that love brings you. You are sowing the seeds of your hopes.

LEFT: *In the Season of Hope, as with spring and new growth, you should gently open your heart to the love that surrounds you.*

OPPOSITE: *Look deeply into your partner's eyes and listen to his or her heart.*

Love, when it is fresh, fills and feeds your soul and allows you to be innocent for a while, enraptured by the pulse of your heart. You hope, against hope, that this is in answer to your dreams and that this will take you to where you want to be. It is the nature of love to hope, and this is the season to believe and to act to fulfil that hope.

Preparation

Spend some time thinking about all the things that you would like to share with the person you love, the things that you have dreamed of that you would like to happen.

Think about what the person in your life has said during the day, such as what he told you about himself or what has been discussed. Did you listen to his needs? Did you truly understand the meaning? In this season people often become caught up in the whirl of love and misunderstand each other, or they may become disconnected from reality and exist in a dream world. You must make the effort to move away from dreaming into the world that exists about you, even if it is sometimes harsh. This is a season of listening.

Here you are laying the seeds for the future. You are setting the boundaries, the expectations of the burgeoning relationship. If you do not hear what the other person dreams of, if you do not hear his thoughts, then you will never know whether the path that you walk will take you closer to or further away from that person. Only by listening to what the other person's ideas and needs, are you able truly to give your heart to him. Later in the relationship you will be able to listen more easily, but now you need to be careful and patient.

Meditation

This is a meditation for listening and looking, reminding you that there is always more to see. You will never see all there is to see on a beach, in a tree or in a person. You must always be looking harder because there is something extraordinary hidden in every tiny crevice and even in the darkest corners.

1 Kneel, sitting on your heels, with your toes behind you and your back and neck straight. Rest your hands on your thighs or knees. This should feel relatively comfortable. Close your eyes and breathe slowly. Relax and try to empty your mind. Start by listening to the noises around you. Try to pick out each distinguishing sound. Listen harder. What background sounds can you notice? Perhaps there are some which you were not even aware of before.

2 Now take three slow breaths and empty your mind again. Open your eyes and look in front of you. Do not move your head, just see what is in front of your eyes. Look closer and notice the textures, the shadows and the patterns hiding even in a simple wall. Take three slow breaths and empty your mind before moving. You can repeat this mental exercise while eating, noticing all the tastes in each mouthful of food, or while dressing, noticing all the textures as they brush against your skin.

Maypole Love Charm

This is an ancient sign of fertility and the joining of the male and female together. People danced around the maypole during the spring May Day festival, with children interweaving coloured ribbons, symbolizing the interwoven nature of man and woman.

This love charm is a symbol of the beginning and hope of spring. Make this small version as a love token to signify the hope that the lives of you and your loved one will be interlinked in the coming cycle. This charm demonstrates your intention to work together with the other person, to weave your paths together, so that both your dreams are fulfilled.

You will need

Straight wooden stick
Knife
Four coloured ribbons
Thread or wool (yarn)
Beads, pendants or stones for decoration

ABOVE: *Select ribbons that are appropriate for the person who will receive the maypole. The maypole is symbolic of lives entwining.*

LEFT: *The Maying festival has been enjoyed for centuries.* Come Join in the Maypole Dance *by Henry John Yeend King (1855–1924).*

1 Think about the wood you want to use for the Maypole and then find a fallen branch from a tree. A relatively straight stick will be easier to weave around. Smooth the wood, either by cutting off the nodules or by stripping off the bark. Select four coloured ribbons, keeping in mind the person you intend to give this to. Each ribbon can also represent a season in the cycle of love.

2 Take the lengths of ribbon and secure them around the top of the stick using the thread or wool (yarn). Hold the stick firmly in place and lay out the ribbons in the four directions. You will want to wind the north and south ribbons clockwise and the east and west ribbons anti-clockwise around the wood.

3 Weave two sets of adjacent ribbons together as shown; north ribbon over the west one and the south ribbon over the east one.

4 Repeat weaving the ribbons around the stick crossing alternate, adjacent pairs, in a continuous pattern until you reach the base.

5 Secure the ends with thread or wool. Now, either leave the ribbon ends free, or tie beads, pendants or stones into them to make the charm a unique and special gift.

Wishing Stone Love Charm

In the Season of Hope you strike out towards your dreams, wishing they would come true. A wishing stone is an object that can contain all of your wishes and those of the person you love, the little ones and the big ones, holding them together in one symbolic place.

As a love charm, a wishing stone reminds you of the wishes you share with another and that you have remembered them. By using a wishing stone as a talisman to hold your wishes, you are taking the first step towards bringing them into reality. When you present the love charm, tell the person you love about the wishes it holds and invite him or her to fill it with their wishes, too. Listen to your partner's wishes. Perhaps each of you can fill the stone with new wishes as they come to you. Whenever you see the stone, remember each one of the wishes it contains, and think about how you might make one of them come true.

You will need

- Stone
- Pen and paper
- Paintbrush
- Coloured enamel paint
- Re-usable adhesive

LEFT: *The wishing stone is an ancient charm for making your dreams come true. Often a person would make a wish as he dropped the stone into the sea or a wishing well.*

1 Find a stone that you feel would make a good object to remember wishes by. Think about what the stone is made of, its shape and what marks and texture it has. Think of three wishes you have, wishes you would like to share with a special person. Try and imagine some patterns or shapes that remind you of those thoughts. Sketch them on paper. Keep the symbols of your wishes simple and bold; perhaps the outline of shapes or animals.

2 Paint the pattern on to the stone using enamel paints in colours you feel that the person you love would appreciate. Think of other patterns that you feel the person you are giving this to would like to see. Try and paint the stone all over its surface using all the colours. When you have finished painting, or if you need to pause during the painting, place the stone on a piece of re-usable adhesive to hold it upright.

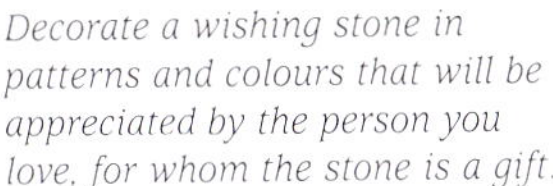

Decorate a wishing stone in patterns and colours that will be appreciated by the person you love, for whom the stone is a gift.

Season of Passion

When you can see and hear the other person for who he or she is, when you are completely open with him or her and it is reciprocal, then you are in a safe place to express the passion that fills your heart. This is the season of heat, of dance, of rapture and cries of joy. This is the season where you can leap into your dreams wholeheartedly, where you can reap the benefits of sharing and listening. Now you know the other person and know that your hearts beat to the same rhythm.

This is the season when two people move as one, when your passion for life spills over. Passion and love can be forces of tremendous change and it often takes courage to ride this season to its peak. Never be afraid to express your feelings, or embrace the other person's feelings with joy. When there are moments of disharmony, always remember the hopes you shared before, and remember how to listen and not to judge. At this time, if it is appropriate, you may decide to follow the heat of passion in lovemaking. This is a period when you give with every part of your being, without any regrets, guilt or mindless disrespect, but with honour and beauty.

In this time of rising passion, you lay your soul bare to the other person. You find the courage to show your vulnerability because this is the only way to share your deepest self with him or her. Sometimes when you feel vulnerable, you can put up defences, as the ego reluctantly relinquishes control of the heart and your past wounds, if still healing, are revealed. With these defences there is often irrational anger, a closing down and withdrawal of the person. You must always respect someone when you walk close to painful places. Let him or her be angry and offer understanding. Love understands grief, as it is part of the natural cycle.

In this season you must be mindful of the joy and the pain in the places where you light the fires of passion.

LEFT: *In the Season of Passion, as with nature flowering in summer, you become gloriously alive, your love can grow and you express your love with every fibre of your being.*

OPPOSITE: *Now is the time to open your heart and release your passion.*

Preparation

With passion comes expression. You must let your body, the truest expression of your soul, easily demonstrate your feelings. Try to become used to expressing yourself openly, in words and deeds. Be confident in your feelings, no one else may judge them. They are not right or wrong. Let your body language become more expressive.

Dance to some music you enjoy and feel comfortable moving your body. Experiment with moving different parts of it. Start by dancing with the head and neck, then with the shoulders. Bring in your arms, elbows, wrists and fingertips so that your whole upper body is in motion. Then introduce the movement of the spine, the sway of your hips, the thousand ways to move your legs and feet, even your toes. If you cannot move some parts of your body, move as much as you are able to. Do not be self-conscious. Just let your whole body express your feelings with the music. Dance for no one but yourself, just becoming comfortable with every pore of your body speaking your heart.

When you are with others be conscious of their physical presence; can you sense what they need? Would they benefit from a hug or a touch of hands? If you find it difficult to sense intuitively what might be appropriate, then do not be afraid to ask. Touch is one of the most important gifts we have to offer, by touching someone we remind them that they belong; that they are wanted and loved in this world. Be aware of your own needs, too. Speak up when you want a hug or even a massage. By asking for physical attention, you open the door for others to open up their hearts and express their love in a physical way.

Spend some time remembering the feeling of the person you love, retrace his or her skin in your mind. If you want to, spend some time together, both of you with your eyes closed. Run your fingers over each other, tracing the outline and contours of your faces. Then, when you are apart, see if you can recall the contours of their body.

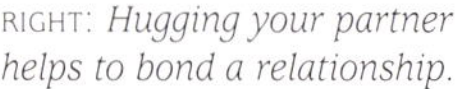

RIGHT: *Hugging your partner helps to bond a relationship.*

LEFT: *Dancing encourages freedom of expression.*

Meditation

This meditation is to aid relaxation and is designed to remind you of the sensation of your own body. Everyone is unique and you should take pleasure from this difference and offer it with joy. Play some relaxing music while performing this mediation to feel the full benefit.

1 Lie down on the floor, with something soft, such as a blanket or rug, beneath your back. Lie relaxed with your hands by your sides. Close your eyes, concentrate and try to feel your body. Notice which parts feel slightly tense and which feel completely relaxed.

2 Start with your toes. Breathing in, clench them up as hard as you can and then as you breathe out, release them. Next, do the same with your ankles. As you breathe in, tense them to bring your feet off the floor, and then relax as you breathe out.

3 Work your way slowly up your body, clenching and relaxing your knees, your thighs, your bottom, your stomach, your fingers and your shoulders, all the way up to your head. Finally, try to clench the scalp of your head and then relax it. Take a long, slow breath and relax. Notice your body again. If there are parts which still feel a little tense, repeat the exercise with them.

As you grow more proficient, you will be able to relax parts of your body more easily. This exercise also heightens the awareness of the body, helping you to feel it more intimately.

Garland Love Charm

Flowers and garlands have been used by many cultures to signify the eternal bond between two people, a circle that unites them. A garland of flowers and berries is especially significant, as both are signs of passion and fertility.

Think about which flowers and berries are in season and which you would like to weave into a garland. This garland can also be made into a crown.

It was customary for lovers to leave a garland on the door of their beloved on the first day of summer. Couples used to wear crowns of flowers on their marriage day, and it is still traditional for a bride today to wear some kind of floral headdress. The garland could also be a necklace or used as a decorative wall hanging.

When you give your love charm, tell the person you love how you feel about the bond that you share and what this garland means to you.

You will need

- Branches of leaves
- Flowers
- Ferns or other foliage
- Garden wire
- Garden string or wool (yarn)

LEFT: *The giving of a garland of flowers is an ancient summer custom throughout the world. The garland is a symbol of fertility and of the joining of two people into a single, unbroken, eternal circle of life.*

1 Collect branches of leaves and flowers, but always thank the tree or plant that gave you its fruit. You may also want to collect some berries, ferns or other foliage for the garland. Pull the length of garden wire into a circle and wrap the ends together to secure it. Take a branch and weave it around the circle. If it is not very flexible tie it into shape using the string or wool (yarn).

2 Moving around the circle, weave the branches around, and secure them where necessary with the string. Use the longer, greener branches first and then add the smaller flowers and plants. As you fold a new flower into the garland, think about what it signifies to you and what you would like the garland to bring to the person you are making it for.

3 Repeat this process until you have used up all your foliage and flowers and you are happy with the garland. Present it to the one you love and explain all the thoughts and feelings you have woven into its branches.

Eternity Band Love Charm

As a symbol of the bond that you share with a person you can present him or her with an eternity band. This is a wristband that is tied on and, if possible, never removed until it wears through. It is made as a single circle and then cut in half; each person then wears one half of the band, signifying how the two people are one in their hearts. This is a very potent sign and you should think carefully whether it is the right time for you to share this with someone.

When you present this charm to someone you love, you may want to do so with some ceremony, for example during a meal, in the atmosphere of a lighted candle or in a special place. Tell your lover your feelings and your passions as you present the charm and explain what this eternity band signifies to you. If he accepts the gift, cut the band in half between knots using scissors. Each of you can then tie the other person's band into place and, if it feels right, seal the final knot with a kiss.

You will need

Beads, shells, any other items
Leather thong or lace

1 Begin by spending some time quietly, preparing your thoughts and capturing the intent with which you wish to fill the eternity band. Gather up small beads and shells and any other charms that you feel should be a part of the band.

2 Cut the length of thong or lace so that you can wrap it roughly three times around your wrist. Leave about 2cm (¾in) and tie a knot at one end of the thong. Think about the pattern that you want to make.

3 Begin threading on the beads and charms. Group the beads together by tying a knot in the thong or lace, then thread on the beads. Tie another knot to secure them into the pattern. Do this at frequent intervals.

4 When you have only 2.5–5cm (1–2in) left, tie the last knot to secure the charms, then tie the two ends together.

5 Present the charm to your partner, cut the wristband in half and tie one half around one another's wrists.

Season of Fulfilment

Once passion has risen, peaked and found its natural balance, you will find there is a huge and wonderful space created between the person you love and yourself. It is a space where you are nurtured and where possibilities exist you had not even dreamed of before.

This is a time when you can reflect on your journey. You have the time to learn from all those mistakes in the past seasons. You may realize that you have reached a place which was not part of your dream and in which you must now find peace.

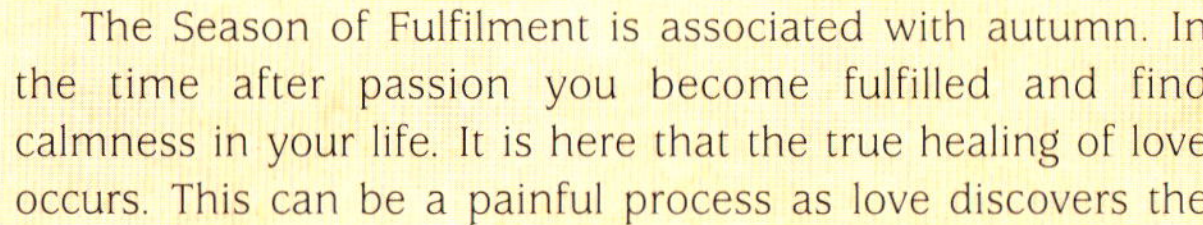

The Season of Fulfilment is associated with autumn. In the time after passion you become fulfilled and find calmness in your life. It is here that the true healing of love occurs. This can be a painful process as love discovers the deeper aspects of your heart and the healing of old wounds occurs.

Now you must also accept that this contentment is transitory. It will not last and should not last. If you are content for too long, you forget your dreams and stop the cycle of love from carrying on. If you get stuck here, if the cycle stops, so too will love and you may wake up one day and find it has left you completely.

In the time of fulfilment you are rejoicing in the journey so far, but also preparing for new dreams and letting go of old ones which you find you no longer yearn for.

It is a time of acceptance, honesty and the knowledge that all things change and that some things must perish for others to live.

LEFT: *In the Season of Fulfilment, as in autumn, some things wither and die to make way for new growth.*

The highest love of all finds its fulfilment not in what it keeps, but in what it gives.
Father Andrew SDC

Preparation

This is the season for looking at yourself carefully in the mirror, noticing the changes that have happened and accepting who you are and where you are.

Spend time alone thinking about what your dreams and hopes were at the beginning of the cycle, the time when you were last dreaming about who you are and what you want to do and be. Think about whether you have fulfilled those dreams or whether they still have meaning for you. Write down those dreams that no longer represent what you desire. Now think about yourself and how you have changed. Are there things that you don't like about yourself? What things are you glad to have gained from love? Write down all the things that you feel you have lost. As you write down each one, try to remember one thing you have gained that replaces it.

Think about and value the self-knowledge that you will inevitably acquired during the cycle. By opening your heart to another, you have looked deeper into yourself.

Finally, take a long look at your habits. Are you fixed in your ways? Are there habits that prevent you from accepting new aspects of your relationship? Write down all those habits and consciously make an effort to let go of them, and with each one think of a possibility that may open up by doing things differently.

Take all those words and put them to rest. Either build a fire for them, or bury them, or throw them into the sea or a lake. As you do so, remember all the wonderful gifts that the relationship has brought you.

LEFT: *As you reflect on the past cycle, make a note of your reassessment.*

Meditation

As you reach a time of change, you often find you become tense and full of dark thoughts as you resist the need to change. You often become angry, not wanting to let the cycle move on, but preferring to keep the status quo. This is a meditation for releasing any dark clouds of anger or frustration and replacing them with warmth and light, so that you are ready to accept whatever is ahead. It is especially good if practised first thing in the morning.

1 Stand with your feet shoulder-width apart and parallel. Keep your back straight, head up and your arms relaxed in front of you. Bend your knees slightly and close your eyes. Feel heavy in your body, sink your weight downwards so that you are firmly connected with the ground.

2 Bring your arms up in a wide circle and breathe in slowly and deeply through your nose. As you do so, imagine that the air you breathe in is full of white light, happiness and all the bright possibilities that the day holds before you.

3 Turn your palms downwards and bring your arms down in front of you, breathing out through your mouth. As you do so, imagine the air you are expelling is grey and dark, full of all the worries and frustrations of the past day or moments before. Let your hands come to rest at your sides again and repeat the exercise twice more.

Protective Love Charm

In many cultures giving a cloak or scarf signifies the offer of protection, that the person giving will be responsible for the wellbeing of the other.

You can give a decorated piece of fabric that symbolizes a cloak as a love charm to signify that you will always respect the other person. You are there should he need you, but equally you will remain folded away if he needs to be alone.

The size of the fabric can be large enough for physical warmth – perhaps you could find a real jacket to decorate – or it can be as small as a token handkerchief or scarf as it is here. A cloak has a deep connection with the blankets you were wrapped in as a baby: they offered peace to the heart. You can remind someone through touching the cloak or fabric token that you are always there when you are needed.

Think about the pattern or decorations to use on the fabric. For example, do you want an emblem signifying your love in the centre of the piece, or do you want to decorate only the borders? When you have finished preparing the fabric give it to the person you love as a folded parcel. Let him unfold it and place it around his shoulders, or accept it as a token of your intentions. Explain to him what your thoughts were while making it and what your feelings are now.

You will need

- Square of fabric
- Soft pencil
- Needle and thread
- Small pieces of fabric, beads and charms
- Paintbrush
- Fabric paints or embroidery thread (floss)

LEFT: *Giving a protective love charm symbolizes the intention to respect your partner through life.*

1 Select the material and colour carefully, imagining what will feel the most warming to the recipient.

2 Draw out the pattern on the cloth, using a pencil. Think about the images and symbols.

3 Sew on the pieces of fabric you have chosen. You can also tie on beads and other charms if you feel they are needed.

4 Now use either fabric paints or embroidery thread (floss) to fill in the pattern.

Talking Stick Love Charm

The talking stick is a Native American charm to help people communicate during difficult times. It can be made of any material, although traditionally it was a carved wooden stick.

A talking stick love charm can be made for any unspoken problem. Use it as a way of moving forward in a relationship, accepting changes as they are encountered. To use a talking stick, place it in front of both of you. If one of you wishes to speak, you can then pick up the stick. The other person must listen intently and respectfully in silence. When the speaker has finished he or she replaces the stick on the ground for the other person to pick up and speak. Here, for this Season of Fulfilment and healing, the stick is made as a rolled scroll of paper.

Consider what inscription you would like to put on the scroll. This will be hidden during the time you are talking and, after you have both said what it is that you need to, the scroll or talking stick can be burnt to symbolize that the issue is now forgotten.

You will need

- Coloured paints or pencils
- Paintbrush
- Paper or cardboard
- Coloured ribbon or wool (yarn)

LEFT: *Burning the talking stick signifies that the problem has been discussed, released and can be forgotten.*

1 Using the coloured pencils or paints, draw out the inscription on the paper. Spend time designing and choosing the words or symbols, remembering that they indicate talking and listening to the person you love.

2 Paint on the design and let it dry. As you paint each brushstroke, think about listening to the person you love, and about letting go of the problem so that you can both live without its shadow over you.

3 Roll up the paper into a scroll, and secure it with some wool (yarn) or ribbon. The symbols along with your intentions are now bound with the roll of the charm.

4 Present the charm to the person you love and suggest how it may be used. If you both feel the need to talk about something that is difficult, use it as described, so that one listens while the other speaks, holding the stick. When you both feel you have finished, throw the talking stick on to a fire and watch the flames devour it, symbolizing the healing and end to the issue.

Final Word

Love is a gift that we all share, as friends, as family, as all creatures living together on this wonderful Earth. At every moment we are given a chance to express that connection, whether it be hugging a friend or offering what we have to those who go without.

To love someone is a truly precious and joyous feeling, but it is also one that will constantly challenge you to listen to and learn from. Love is a living thing. When you stop listening and give up learning then the beauty of it withers and fades.

Love charms are gifts, tools and special places where you can remind yourself of the beauty that you share with someone, or reawaken something that has shrivelled up from neglect. They can help turn your dreams into a reality and take you on in the cycle to create more dreams and more special moments in your life.

It sometimes takes courage and determination to follow the cycle of love. You must always be listening to the voice of your heart so that you can move ever forwards towards your dream. There may be times when you must weep for what you have lost, but there will be other times when you will cry out with joy at what you have gained. Everyone walks the cycle of love, and its changing seasons carry them onwards to happiness and the life of their dreams.

Love charming is an art that everyone possesses; they are born with its knowledge beating inside them. You can practise this art of bringing love to everyone around you as part of the everyday world. In so doing, you become the warm, loving person that you truly are at heart.

May you walk a path of beauty and love every moment of your life and so live the life of your dreams.

LEFT: *The lovers,* Paolo and Francesca da Rimini, *1867 by Dante Gabriel Rossetti (1828–1882).*

OPPOSITE: Venus Verticordia, *1864–68 by Dante Gabriel Rossetti.*

Rune	Letter	Name	Table of Rune Symbols for Love Charms
ᚠ	F	Feoh	Wealth, riches and blessings for a new beginning
ᚢ	U	Ur	The strength and perseverance of the wild ox
ᚦ	Th	Thorn	Protection of thorns around the heart
ᚨ	A	Ansuz	Speaking and telling of charms and dreams
ᚱ	R	Rad	Turning the wheel and cycle of love
ᚲ	K	Ken	Bringing the light of understanding and acceptance
ᚷ	G	Gyfu	The giving and sharing of equals
ᚹ	W	Wyn	Joy of life when you are walking the path to your dreams
ᚺ	H	Hagal	Destruction of the old and letting go of the past
ᚾ	N	Nyd	The need for love, which burns in your heart
ᛁ	I	Is	Sudden endings, frozen and broken in a moment
ᛃ	J	Jera	Celebrating the seasons of love
ᛇ	Z	Eihwaz	Eternity of love and its cycle of creation, death and renewal
ᛈ	P	Peorth	The freedom of choice to make your own choices
ᛉ	X	Elhaz	Protection and resistance against ill-intended actions
ᛊ	S	Sigel	The sun at dawn, bringing light to the dark places in your life
ᛏ	T	Tiwaz	Justice and truth everywhere beneath the spinning sky
ᛒ	B	Beorc	The birth of fertile new beginnings
ᛖ	E	Ehwaz	The loyalty and faithfulness of the horse
ᛗ	M	Man	Connection of each person as human beings on Earth
ᛚ	L	Lagu	Water to help your life and love grow
ᛜ	Ng	Ing	Spreading the boundless light of your heart out into the world
ᛟ	O	Odal	Creating a space in your life which you can call your own
ᛞ	D	Dag	Welcoming in bright intentions and warding off dark ones

Tree	Letter	Old Name	Table of Trees for Love Charms
Birch	B	Beth	Sweep away the dark places in your heart to allow something new to grow
Rowan	L	Luis	The protection of fire against the dark
Ash	N	Nion	Force of creation allowing you to form reality from your dreams
Alder	F	Fearn	Emotional strength and perseverance
Willow	S	Saille	Flowing, cleansing water of healing
Hawthorn	H	Huath	Birth of possibilities and hope
Oak	D	Duir	Doorway through to understanding of the heart
Holly	T	Tinne	Never-ending watchfulness
Hazel	C	Coll	Listening to your dreams and taking the initiative to make them happen
Bramble	M	Muin	Bringing about change in your life and dreams
Ivy	G	Gort	Determination and strength in walking around the cycle of love
Reed	Ng	Ngetal	Speaking and writing words from your heart
Elder	R	Ruis	Calling the magic of love into your life
Apple	Q	Quert	Sharing the limitless love in the world
Blackthorn	St	Straif	Projection of your heart and feelings out into the world
Elm	A	Ailm	Growing onwards and upwards to rise above the difficulties in life
Gorse	O	Onn	Hope of what love will bring
Heather	U	Ur	Renewing and refreshing old or tired love
Poplar	E	Eadha	Directing your feelings towards a particular person or place in your life
Yew	I	Iubhar	Learning from the past and letting it go

Index

A
Alma-Tadema, Sir Lawrence 9
animals 20
apple 15, 18, 63
aromatherapy oils 19
art of love 26–7
ash 63

B
beech 15
birch 15, 63
blackthorn 63
bramble 63
broomstick 17
Burne-Jones, Edward 11

C
cha-li 14
courting charms 14–15
Cowper, Frank Cadogan 13
Cupid Delivering Psyche (Burne-Jones) 11

D
dance 24, 46
diamond 21
dove 20
dream catcher charm 32–3
dream space charm 34–5
dreams, season of 28–32

E
elder 63
elm 63
eternity band charm 50–1

F
fairytale charms 12–13
fertility symbols 14
flute 10
food 14, 17
fulfilment 52–5

G
garland charm 48–9
geasa 10
gorse 63

H
hair, lock of 16
hawthorn 63
hazel 15, 63
heather 63
holly 18, 63
hope, 36–9

I
inscription 22
ivy 63

J
jewellery 21, 34

K
Keane, Bill 8
Kiss, The (Alma-Tadema) 9
knots 23

L
lavender 19
legendary charms 10–11
letters, words and 22, 62–3
lightning 21
lily 19
love, cycle of 27

M
marriage 16–17
Maypole charm 40–1
meditation 31, 39, 47, 55
menstrual cycle 25
mistletoe 18
monogram 22
moon 25
mythology 19–20
  Celtic 10, 20, 23, 25
  Greek 11, 20
  Indian 20
  Native American 10, 32, 58
  Norse 20, 22
  Roman 11, 26
  Sioux 10
  Tibetan 21

N
Norse alphabet 22

O
oak 63

P
Paolo and Francesca da Rimini (Rossetti) 60
passion 44–7
pearl 21
poplar 63
protective love charm 56

R
Rapunzel (Cowper) 13
receiving 9
reed 63
rings 16
Romeo and Juliet (Dicksee) 7
rose 19
Rossetti, Dante Gabriel 10, 60, 61
rowan 63
ruby 21
runes 22, 62

S
seal 20
seasons and cycles 25, 26–32, 36–9, 40, 44–7, 52–5
shapes 23
Sleeping Beauty, The (Spence) 12
squash, symbolic 17
stones 21
swan 20
symbols 14, 18–25
  animals 20
  body and motion 24
  flowers 19
  patterns 23
  seasons and cycles 25
  stones 21
  table of 62–3
  trees 18, 63
  words and letters 22, 62

T
tables 62–3
talking stick charm 58–9
Mirror of Venus, The (Burne-Jones) 11
touch 24
trees 10, 14–15, 18, 63
Tristan and Iseult Drinking the Love Potion (Rossetti) 10
Tristan and Isolde (Turnbull) 8

V
Venus Verticordia (Rossetti) 61

W
Waterhouse, John 60
wheel of the year 25
willow 18, 63
wishing stone charm 42–3
words 22, 62–3